Rajat

Poems of the ...

translations from the Chinese

A. C. Graham is a leading authority on Chinese thought, grammar and textual criticism, as well as one of the finest translators of classical Chinese poetry in English. He was Professor of Classical Chinese at the School of Oriental Studies, University of London, until 1988, and has taught and carried out research at a number of other universities throughout the world. His numerous publications include *Chuang-tzu: the Seven Inner Chapters* and the Penguin Classics *Poems of the Late T'ang*. The most recent of his books is *Disputers of the Tao: Philosophical Argument in Ancient China*.

To Gu Meigao
with gratitude

A. C. Graham

Poems of the West Lake

translations
from the Chinese
by
A. C. Graham
with an introduction

wellsweep

ACKNOWLEDGEMENTS

A number of the poems in this book were published in the Chinese-English translation magazine *Renditions* (no. 25, Spring 1986) whose permission to reprint them here is gratefully acknowledged.
The calligraphy for the original texts of the poems and that on the title page and front cover is by Mr Joseph Lo.
The cover ilustration is reproduced from the *Mingkan Shantu Banhua Ji*, Shanghai, 1958, and the inscription on the back cover, describing the 'ten famous sights of West Lake' is from a scroll in a private collection. Other illustrations accompanying the text are from the *Xihu zhi*.

Translation copyright © A. C. Graham

First published in 1990 by
Wellsweep Press
719 Fulham Road
London SW6 5UL

0 948454 07 5 trade edition (laminated cover)
0 948454 57 1 readers' edition (laid paper cover)

All rights reserved: no part of this publication may be reproduced, stored in a retrieval system, or transmitted in any form or by any means, electronic, mechanical, photocopying or otherwise, without the prior written permission of the publisher.

Editor's notes: The original text accompanying the poem on page 11 preserves an alternate reading, *you* for *huai*, although Professor Graham favours the latter in his version.
The Wang Wei in this collection (*hao*: Xianlu) is not to be confused with the Tang dynasty poet whose name is spelt differently in Chinese characters.

Designed and set by Wellsweep
Printed by E & E Plumridge Ltd., Linton, Cambridge

CONTENTS

Introduction / 7

the Tang dynasty

Li Bai / 10
Liu Yuxi / 12
Bai Juyi / four poems / 14

the Song dynasty

Su Shi / four poems / 22
Chen Shidao / 28
Chao Zhongzhi / 30
Xu Fu / 32
Lin Sheng / 34
Yang Wanli / two poems / 36
Wu Weixin / 40
Jiang Kui / 42
Wang Wei / two poems / 44

the Ming dynasty

Shi Jian / 46
Gao Deyang / two poems / 48
Yu Qian / two poems / 52
Wang Shizhen / two poems / 56
Mo Fan / two poems / 60

INTRODUCTION

The West Lake of Hangzhou, one of the famous sights of the Jiangnan region south of the Yangzi, has been a theme of poets for more than one thousand years. When the court of the Song dynasty lost its capital, Kaifeng, to the Nüzhen invaders from the north and fled across the Yangzi, it was at Hangzhou near the river mouth that it chose to settle. As capital of the Southern Song (AD 1127-1279), Hangzhou enjoyed the precarious glory of high culture and military weakness, until the South too fell to barbarian invaders, the Mongols.

In Imperial times you approached the lake from the Yongjin Gate in the city's west wall, and hurried to be back before it shut for the night. Ahead, over Breakoff Bridge (Duanqiao) was, and still is, the White Causeway (Baidi), supposed to have been built by the poet Bai Juyi (772-846) when he was governor of Hangzhou, although he mentions it in his poems as already there. It ends at Lone Hill (Gushan), a little island which can be seen from all directions jutting from the water, itself joined by a bridge to the north shore at West Ridge (Xiling) where the singing girl Su (Su Xiaoxiao, c. AD 500) was buried. The island was the home of the hermit Lin Bu (967-1028), admirer of the winter blossom, the plum, who never went down the causeway to the city. The Su Causeway (Sudi), which cuts across the far side of the lake from north to south, was built by another great poet who was governor of Hangzhou, Su Shi (Su Dongpo, 1037-1101). Beyond, running along the west side of the lake, are wooded hills with two peaks, Beigao (North Peak) and Nangao (South Peak), and the vulture-shaped Feilai which was said to have flown all the way from India. Dotting the hills are Buddhist temples, among them the three India Temples (Tianzhusi), the oldest of which was once more famous than the lake itself, as may be seen from the poem of Li Bai (701-762) which is the earliest translated here. In the grounds of the temples in autumn you could pick up cassia 'buds' (as we call them in English, in fact the immature fruit), and fancy that they had fallen from the moon, where a cassia tree grows beside the multicoloured toad and the lady Chang E who fled to the moon with the herb of immortality, both mentioned in the lyric by Mo Fan. Through the woodlands you can walk to the Qiantang river south of the lake, where every autumn the tidal wave of the Hangzhou Bore comes rushing up from the sea. At the north-west corner of the lake, a reminder of harsh realities, is the shrine of the hero Yue Fei, whose victory at Zhuxianzhen in 1140 briefly revived hopes of recovering the North; he was slandered by the peace party and died in prison two years later. We pass over all glories of Hangzhou which happen not to be mentioned in these poems.

The lake with its causeways and artificial islands is a work of art as well as nature which has taken shape gradually through the centuries; the earliest to write of the bore or the temples of Hangzhou seem hardly to notice it. The first to find words to describe it is Bai Juyi, whose impressions of the West Lake have the freshness of new discovery. Su Shi established what came to be the convention, the vivid glimpse captured in a graceful quatrain, which every Song and Yuan sightseer seems able to throw off without effort. Wang Wei, Gao Deyang and Mo Fan all take their themes from the 'Ten Prospects', the commonly recognised ten best sights, which include 'Lingering snow on Breakoff Bridge', 'Autumn moon on the smooth lake' (to be seen from the south-east of the island), 'The print of the moon in the three pools' (reflections of the moon and the three stone lanterns), as well as two not on the list which became standard, 'Settled snow on Lone Hill' and 'Waves through the pines for nine miles'. During the Ming a few try for something different or deeper, Gao Deyang by his lurid metaphors for a winter dawn, Wang Shizhen by the images of the eternal within the transient which he sees in the pool of Jade Springs Temple (Yuquansi) north-west of the lake.

The Lady of the West (Xi Shi), the beautiful concubine presented by the King of Yue to the King of Wu, two ancient states in this southern region, is a recurrent image of the West Lake when its feminine curves of hill and pavilion are blurred by spring mists. For the transparency of the lake in the clear light of autumn a favourite image is ice in a bowl of white jade, a cliché variously abbreviated ('bowl of ice', 'bowl of jade').

I had the pleasure of drafting these translations during a too short visit to Hangzhou in the early spring of 1984.

A. C. G.

送崔十二遊天竺寺　李白

遠聞天竺寺　夢想遊東越
每年海樹霜　桂子落秋月
送君遊此地　已屬流芳歇
待我來歲行　相隨浮溟渤

Li Bai (701-762)

SEEING OFF TWELFTH SON CUI
ON HIS JOURNEY TO THE INDIA TEMPLE

Once more hearing of the India Temple,
Imagining in dreams I long for eastern Yue.
Each year in the frost on the seacoast trees
The cassia buds drop from the autumn moon.
Saying goodbye as you travel to that land,
I'm already of those whose scent has faded from the air.
Look out for me, next year here I come,
In search of you, floating in from the estuary.

浪淘沙　　劉禹錫

八月濤聲吼地來　頭高數丈觸山回

須臾卻入海門去　卷起沙堆似雪堆

Liu Yuxi (772-842)

NOISE OF BREAKERS IN THE EIGHTH MONTH

In the Eighth Month the noise of breakers comes roaring
                               through the land,
The head a dozen yards high butts the hill and turns.
An instant, and it bends round to enter Sea Gate,
Rolling back heaps of sand like heaps of snow.

钱塘湖春行　白居易

孤山寺北贾亭西，水面初平云脚低。
几处早莺争暖树，谁家新燕啄春泥。
乱花渐欲迷人眼，浅草才能没马蹄。
最爱湖东行不足，绿杨阴里白沙堤。

Bai Juyi (772-846)

WALKING IN SPRING BY WEST LAKE

North of Lone Hill Temple, west of the Jia Pavilion,
The water's surface has just smoothed, the foot of the cloud low.
Wherever you go new-risen orioles jostle for the warmest tree:
What are they after, the newborn swallows that peck
                                        at the spring mud?
A riot of blossoms not long from now will be dazzling to the eye,
The shallow grass can hardly yet submerge the horse's hoof.
Best loved of all, to the east of the lake, where I can never
                                        walk enough,
In the shade of the green willows, the causeway of white sand.

西湖晚歸回望孤山寺贈諸客 白居易

柳湖松島蓮花寺
廬橘子低山雨重
煙波淡蕩搖空碧
到岸請君回首望

晚動歸橈出道場
栟櫚葉戰水風涼
樓殿參差倚夕陽
蓬萊宮在水中央

RETURNING IN THE EVENING FROM WEST LAKE, LOOKING BACK AT LONE HILL ISLAND IN THE DISTANCE

Lake of willows, island of pines, temple of flowering lotus —
In the evening stirring homeward oars we leave the holy ground.
Cumquats droop, the rain on the hill heavy:
Palm leaves shiver, the breeze on the water cool.
Misted waves tossing and turning quiver the blue of the sky,
Towers and roofs in a jagged line lean on the setting sun.
As we come to shore, I beg you, look back and view far off:
The palace of the Isle of Immortals in the centre of the waves.

春题湖上　　白居易

湖上春来如画图　乱峰围绕水平铺
松排山面千重翠　月点波心一颗珠
碧毯线头抽早稻　青罗裙带展新蒲
未能抛得杭州去　一半勾留是此湖

SPRING THEME: ABOVE THE LAKE

Now spring is here the lake seems a painted picture,
Unruly peaks all round the edge, the water spread out flat.
Pines in ranks on the face of the hills, a thousand layers of green:
The moon centred on the heart of the waves, just one pearl.
Threadends of an emerald-green rug, the extruding
                                        paddy-shoots:
Sash of a blue damask skirt, the expanse of new reeds.
If I cannot bring myself yet to put Hangzhou behind me,
Half of what holds me here is on this lake.

忆江南　　白居易

江南忆　最忆是杭州　山寺月中寻桂子　郡亭枕上看潮头　何日更重游

REMEMBERING JIANGNAN

      Remembered of Jiangnan,
The best remembered is Hangzhou.
In a hill temple in the moonlight searching for cassia buds,
In the State Pavilion, head on pillow, watching the tidal wave.
When will be the day that I shall roam again?

饮湖上初晴后雨

苏轼

水光潋滟晴方好

山色空濛雨亦奇

欲把西湖比西子

淡妆浓抹总相宜

Su Shi (1037-1101)

DRINKING BY THE LAKE:
CLEAR SKY AT FIRST, THEN RAIN

The shimmer of light on the water is the play of sunny skies,
The blur of colour across the hills is richer still in rain.
If you wish to compare the lake in the west to the Lady of the West,
Lightly powdered or thickly smeared the fancy is just as apt.

六月二十七日望湖楼醉书　苏轼

黑云翻墨未遮山，白雨跳珠乱入船。
卷地风来忽吹散，望湖楼下水如天。

放生鱼鳖逐人来，无主荷花到处开。
水枕能令山俯仰，风船解与月裴回。

SIXTH MONTH, 27TH DAY:
WRITTEN WHILE DRUNK ON LAKE PROSPECT TOWER

1

Swirled ink of black cloud has not yet covered the hills,
Jumping pearls of white rain riotously enter the boat.
A wind to curl the earth up comes, in an instant blows them away,
And under Lake Prospect Tower water seems sky.

2

The fish and turtles it's forbidden to catch come as near you
                                                      as they please,
The lotus blossoms no one owns open wherever you go.
Pillowed on water you can order the hills to tilt up, tilt down.
The boat in the breeze has got the knack of ambling round
                                                      with the moon.

望海楼晚景

苏轼

横风吹雨入楼斜

北观应须好句夸

雨过潮平江海碧

电光时掣紫金蛇

EVENING VIEW FROM SEA PROSPECT TOWER

A transverse wind blows the rain aslant into the tower.
(Grand sights demand you show off with a pretty line.)
The rain passes, the tide smooths, river and sky are blue.
Flashes of lightening at intervals pluck a snake of purple gold.

十七日觀潮

陳師道

漫漫平沙走白虹

瑤臺失手玉杯空

晴天搖動清江底

晚日浮沉急浪中

Chen Shidao (1053-1101)

WATCHING THE TIDAL WAVE

Overflowing the level sand a white rainbow runs.
Up in heaven a hand has slipped, a cup of jade has spilled.
The clear sky shifts and quivers at the bottom of the limpid stream,
The evening sun sinks and floats inside the hurrying waves.

送人游江南

寇冲之

酒金门外断红尘 衣锦城边着白蘋

不到西湖看山色 定应未可作诗人

Chao Zhongzhi (c. 1090)

SEEING SOMEONE OFF ON HIS TRAVELS TO
JIANGNAN

Outside Yongjin Gate you'll be free of the red dust,
Nearby the city dressed in brocades you'll wear
                              white duckweed flowerets.
Until you come to West Lake and see the colours of the hills,
Say what you will you're not yet ripe to call yourself a poet.

春游湖

徐俯

双飞燕子几时回 夹岸桃花蘸水开

春雨断桥人不度 小舟撑出柳阴来

Xu Fu (1075-1141)

SPRING EXCURSION ON THE LAKE

The swallows flying in couples, when will they be back?
On the flanking shores the peach-buds dip in the water and open.
At Breakoff Bridge in the spring rain where no one passes by
A little boat comes punted out from the shadow of the willows.

题临安邸 林升

山外青山楼外楼 西湖歌舞几时休

暖风熏得游人醉 直把杭州作汴州

Lin Sheng (c. 1180)

AT AN INN IN HANGZHOU

Beyond the hills blue hills, beyond the mansions mansions —
To song and dance on the West Lake when will there be an end?
Idlers fuddled on the fumes of the warm breeze
Will turn Hangzhou that rises into Kaifeng that fell.

昭君怨 咏荷上雨 杨万里

午梦扁舟花底，香满西湖烟水。急雨打篷声，梦初惊。

却是池荷跳雨，散了真珠还聚。聚作水银窝，泻清波。

Yang Wanli (1127-1206)

INTONING TO THE RAIN ON THE LOTUS

(to the air *Plaint of Zhaojun*)

Dreaming at noon in a little boat, flowers overhead.
A scent pervades West Lake mist and water.
Noise of a rush of rain beating the sail —
From dream just startled.

But on the lotus of the pool, in the dance of raindrops,
The pearls that scattered gather again,
Gather to make quicksilver puddles,
Leaking into the clear waves.

秋山

楊萬里

梧葉新黃柿葉紅

夏蕉猶栢與丹楓

只言山色秋蕭索

繡出西湖三四峯

AUTUMN HILLS

Sterculia leaves fresh yellow, persimmon leaves red,
Not to mention the rook-black cypress and the maple of cinnabar.
Say if you will the colours of the hills in autumn are melancholy,
On West Lake it decks in brocades all the peaks along the shore.

苏堤清明即事

吴惟信

梨花风起正清明

游子寻春半出城

日暮笙歌收拾去

万株杨柳属流莺

Wu Weixin (c. 1250)

THE QINGMING FESTIVAL ON THE SU CAUSEWAY:
WRITTEN THE SAME DAY

A breeze rises in the pear blossoms, today it's Qingming.
Sightseers in search of spring have half emptied the city.
When the sun goes down pan-pipe and song have all been
                                                gathered away,
And the thousands of willows belong to the gliding oriole.

湖上寓居雜詠　　姜夔

層層蘆葦望眼寬

荷花荷葉遍闌干

遊人去後無歌鼓

白水青山生晚寒

Jiang Kui (1155-1221)

MISCELLANEOUS VERSES WHILE LODGING BY THE LAKE

Wherever you go a pillared hall wide open to the view.
Lotus blossoms, lotus leaves, come over the balustrades.
After the last strollers have gone, no songs and drums.
From white water and green hills, the evening chill creeps in.

平湖秋月　王洧

萬頃寒光一夕鋪，鸞峰遙度西風去，桂子紛紛照玉壺。

斷橋殘雪

望湖亭外半青山，跨水修梁影亦寒，待伴痕邊分草綠，鶴驚辭玉啄闌干

Wang Wei (c. 1250)

AUTUMN MOON ON THE SMOOTH LAKE

A myriad acres of cold beams spread out all night long:
Where the wheel of ice proceeds, not a trace of cloud.
On the vulture's peak you can guess from afar that
                                  the west wind is chill,
Helter-skelter the cassia buds dot the bowl of jade.

LINGERING SNOW ON BREAKOFF BRIDGE

Beyond Lake Prospect Belvedere, half the hillside green.
On the long bridge straddling the water, in shadow it's colder still.
Beside a patch it took for its mate, perceiving the green of grass,
A crane astonished by smashed white jade pecks at the balustrade.

寄杭州友人 史鉴

西湖三日水初生 重叠青山接郡城

记得扁舟载春酒 满江花影乱啼莺

Shi Jian (Ming dynasty)

TO A FRIEND IN HANGZHOU

On West Lake at the lakeside the water begins to grow.
Layer above layer the spring hills run up from the city walls.
I remember when, in a little boat, loaded with spring wine,
With shadows of flowers all over us we listened to the
                                                        oriole sing.

孤山霁雪 高得赐

山头白石六苍铺 水面青：一簟狐
翠风抟云朝灵阙 玉鳌警日出冰壶
梅花正好冲寒探 竹叶何妨踏冻沽
千载林逋留胜迹 总因佳境在西湖

Gao Deyang (1368-1398)

SETTLED SNOW ON LONE HILL ISLAND

On the white stone of the hilltop six-cornered blossoms spread.
On the blue-black of the water's surface, one solitary topknot.
A purple wind moulds the cloud, the shell of morning cracks:
A white jade turtle lifts the sun out of the bowl of ice.
Plum blossom there's no better time to pick than braving the cold:
Bamboo leaf wine why shouldn't we tread a frozen path to buy?
If Lin Bu left a mark to last a thousand years
It's all because the finest views are here on West Lake.

九里雲松 高得暘

九里青雲一徑開
喬松萬樹總良材
雲氣直從天際去
濤聲長傳海門來
人行道上依稀覺
子落僧房點嫩苔
山水清暉增偉概
托根原不愧相德

CLOUDY PINETOPS FOR NINE MILES

Thousands of trunks of lofty pine, all of it noble timber.
Through nine miles of layered shadow a single path opens.
Its puff of cloud goes straight from the India Temple,
Its noise of waves comes all the way alongside Sea Gate.
Men travelling the road cling to the dense shade,
Cones dropping at monks' feet speckle the tender moss.
To the radiance of hill and water they lend grandeur.
These planted roots would not disgrace the pinelands of Zulai.

夏日憶西湖 于謙

涌金門外柳如煙

西子湖頭水拍天

玉腕罷裙雙蕩槳

鴛鴦飛近採蓮船

Yu Qian (1398-1457)

ON A SUMMER DAY REMEMBERING WEST LAKE

Outside Yongjin Gate the willows are like smoke,
On the Lady of the West's lake the water pats the sky.
Arms jade-white and damask-skirted couples wave the oar,
Mandarin duck and drake fly near the lotus-pickers' boat.

岳忠武王祠　于谦

匹马南来渡浙河，汴城官阙远嵯峨。
中兴诸将谁降虏，贫国奸臣主议和。
黄叶古祠寒雨积，青山荒冢白云多。
如何一别朱仙镇，不见将军奏凯歌。

THE SHRINE OF YUE FEI

A single horse come southward forded the Qiantang,
Palace and watchtower of Kaifeng loomed far behind.
Of the patriot generals who would have surrendered
                                          to barbarians?
Traitorous ministers preferred to talk terms.
By the old shrine in the yellow leaves the cold rain makes puddles,
Up the green hill, on the desolate mound, the white clouds spread.
Why was it that, after his triumph on the field of Zhuxianzhen,
We were never to see the Commander-in-chief perform
                                          his victory song?

游南高峰　　王世贞

漫游指点南高峰，踏屐攀跻兴有馀
画里余杭人卖酒，镜中湖曲棹穿花
千岩风出竹邪雨，一径潋阴迳晚霞
最是夜归迷绝岛，疏林灯火傍渔家

Wang Shizhen (1526-1590)

ROAMING ON SOUTH PEAK

Others who came pointed out South Peak as the one —
Tread your grass shoes, tug at the creepers, you never get
                                      nearer the top.
Inside a painting, in Hangzhou, someone has wine for sale:
Within a mirror, at a bend in the lake, an oar thrusts
                                      through flowers.
A thousand half emerging cliffs part the autumn rain,
A single track of faint light seeps through sunset cloud.
Best of all, coming home at night to an out-of-the-way place,
In the sparse woods, to a lighted lamp beside a fisherman's house.

玉泉寺觀魚　　　　王世貞

寺古碑殘不記年　池清媚景且留連
金鱗慣愛初斜日　玉乳長涵太古天
投餌驟時爭作隊　避人深處月初弦
遙將呂梁同魚樂　不負庄生濠上篇

WATCHING THE FISH IN JADE SPRINGS TEMPLE

Zhuangzi and Hui Shi were strolling on the Bridge of the Hao.
Zhuangzi said, 'The minnows swim out so free and easy, that's what
joy is to a fish.'

The temple's old inscription's worn, doesn't record the year.
Charmed by the scene so clear in the pool let's linger for a while.
Golden scales have grown used to loving sunshine when
                                              first it slants:
Froth of white jade for ever steeps a sky from the beginning
                                              of the world.
At the swarming times, tossed a crumb — slices of the red
                                              of morning.
In the deep places, shunning man — crescent new moons.
To make my joy again like the fishes' joy
I say three times over the tale of Zhuangzi on the Hao.

蝶戀花

平湖秋月

莫璠

璧月呈輝湖淥靚　一色琉璃倒浸
山河影　花外瓊宮愈瑩　人間無此
清涼境　笑擷芙蓉乘舴艋　醉擱文
漪　搖動金千頃　欲喚坡仙同賦詠
桂花露溼衣襟冷

Mo Fan (16th century)

Lyrics to the air *Flowers the butterfly loves*

1

AUTUMN MOON ON THE SMOOTH LAKE

A jade-disc moon lights up, the lake is pure and still.
    A glass of one colour
        Drenches the inverted shadow of the river in the hills.
Beyond the flowers the Jasper Palace glints brighter,
Earth has no scene so clear and cool.

With a smile picking the lotus I ride the little boat,
    Drunken scoop up handfuls of ripples,
        Quivering a thousand acres of gold.
Want to call Su Shi the immortal to versify with me,
Damped by the dew on the cassia flowers,
                the collars of our gowns chilled.

蝶恋花　三潭印月　莫璃

秋净澄潭澄见底　五色蟾蜍飞入
法泠水腰熟矖就呼小起　颔珠光
照冰壶里　谁贵此时能有几　遥忆
同欢今夜人千里　试问龙渊深几
许　骑鲸欲共姮娥语

THE PRINT OF THE MOON IN THE THREE POOLS

In the cold depths cleansed by autumn you see right through
                                                              to the floor.
        The toad of five colours
        Flies into the clear chill water.
Fast asleep the black dragon if you call him does not wake,
The light of the pearl beneath his chin glows in the bowl of ice.

To feast this season how often shall we meet again?
        Think, they that shared our joys
        Are tonight a thousand miles away.
The abyss of the dragon, how deep is it would you suppose?
I want to ride down on a whale and talk to the Lady in the Moon.

New from Wellsweep
July 1990:

Plantains in the Rain
the selected Chinese poems of Du Mu (803–52)
Wellsweep Chinese Poets 3

translated by R. F. Burton

This is the first substantial selection of Du Mu's poetry to be made available in English. Du Mu was a poet of the late Tang dynasty, noted for his superb quatrains. Dr Burton has made him sing in English. The translations are accompanied by the Chinese text.

> Picks broke the green-mossed clod.
> It stole a slip of sky.
> White clouds spawn in the depths of the mirror.
> The bright moon dips at the step.

£5.95 (both editions)
96 pp., 7 ill., 210x130 mm, paper, July 1990
trade edition (laminated cover)   0 948454 08 3
readers' edition (laid paper cover)   0 948454 58 X

Order direct, or from good bookshops.

Write for a complete list of Wellsweep publications:

Wellsweep Press
719 Fulham Road
London SW6 5UL
Fax: (071) 731 8009